A play by Melaina Faranda

Illustrated by Rosie Colligan

Contents

Pearson Australia
(a division of Pearson Australia Group Pty Ltd)
707 Collins Street, Melbourne, Victoria 3008
PO Box 23360, Melbourne, Victoria 8012
www.pearson.com.au

2019 2018 2017 2016
10 9 8 7 6 5 4 3 2 1

Text by Melaina Faranda
Illustrations by Rosie Colligan

Publishers: Sabine Bolick, Beth Zeme
Project Managers: Diane Leyman, Michelle Thomas
Lead Editor: Steve Dobney
Editor: Cameron Macintosh
Proofreader: Thalia Kalkipsakis
Designer: Lisa Howard
Senior File & Asset Coordinator: Rob Curulli
Cover art: Rosie Colligan
Printed and bound in Australia by Pegasus Media & Logistics

ISBN 978 1 4886 1312 8

Pearson Australia Group Pty Ltd
ABN 40 004 245 943

Characters

William

(This part may be played by two actors – one in each act.)

Mary

Constable

(a police officer)

Watson

(a guard)

Judge

Act 1: The Courtroom

William Crow is led by the Constable into the Old Bailey courtroom in London, England. It is 1786. William enters the stand before the Judge.

Judge: Your name is William Crow?

William: Yes, that's what they call me. As for the name my mother gave me, I have no way of knowing.

Judge: Where is she now?

William: She's singing with the angels in Heaven. She has been since I was born.

Constable: That's nonsense, Your Honour. These people are thieves, liars and beggars – the lot of them. Crow's mother is dead, but she is not with the angels. You can be sure of that!

Judge: And you are ten years old, William Crow?

William: How would I know?

Constable: Don't give any of your cheek, boy. This one is bad, Your Honour. He spat and hissed like a cat when we came to fetch him.

Judge: What is your work, William Crow?

William: I am a chimney sweep. I was given my name because I'm always as black as a crow.

Judge: What is the charge against him, Constable?

Constable: The boy was caught thieving three items of clothing valued at more than forty shillings.

Judge: What items were stolen?

Constable: He stole a scarf, a fine linen shirt and a woollen coat. The owner of the house, a respectable man, caught him and sent for us.

William: I wouldn't have taken anything if that rich boy hadn't called me a dirty little animal. When I came down from the chimney, black with soot, he said I should be put in a cage to be laughed at!

Judge: What is he talking about, Constable?

Constable: He means the owner's son, who is a fine young gentleman. You can be sure this William Crow is a lying thief. He would best be taken from the streets before he commits greater crimes.

William: That's not true! I had never stolen before. I only wanted to wear clean clothes, because of what that boy said to me!

Judge: Be quiet or you will be sorry.

William: I can't help it, Your Honour. I won't be called a liar.

Judge: You are paid a wage, William Crow?

William: Yes, but my wage is barely enough to buy a crust of bread and a bit of meat. I sleep in my master's cart under a sack. He only gives me work in winter, and turns me out onto the street in summer. I have no work for months until it becomes colder and people begin lighting fires again.

Constable: So he turns to thieving, Your Honour!

Judge: It is true that London is full of lazy good-for-nothing boys who rob honest people.

William: I just wanted to wear clean clothes, like those people.

Judge: Will the boy's master speak a good word for him?

Constable: The man says we're welcome to him. Crow is getting too big to fit up the smaller chimneys and he has started to disobey orders. It is easier for the master to control the younger boys.

William: My master is a cruel man who makes the little ones cry. Johnny is only six, so I told him not to climb up the chimney while it was still hot. His hands and knees would have been burned.

Constable: See how he speaks about his master! I have seen many bad sorts, and this one is a born troublemaker.

Judge: I believe you are right, Constable. He seems to show little respect for his betters. England is best rid of him. I could sentence him to death by hanging.

William: Please, no!

Constable: Be silent, boy.

Judge: I do note this is the first time he has been found guilty of theft in a court. William Crow, I sentence you to transportation for life to the penal colony of Botany Bay.

Constable: Good riddance to him, too.

William: What does transportation for life mean?

Constable: You will be held on a prison ship on the River Thames until you set sail for the new colony. There, you will be a convict for life.

Judge: Next case!

William: No! **Your Honour!**

William is dragged from the court by the Constable.

Act 2: The Voyage

William Crow is aboard a ship of the First Fleet, bound for Australia in 1787.

Mary: For pity's sake, please help this woman. She is ill. Don't you have any sympathy, you devils?

William: It's true, Sir. She needs to be taken up on deck for some fresh air.

Watson: Hold your tongues, both of you. I am the one in charge here. She will stay with the rest of you convicts below. Besides, the food and water stores are running very low. Why would you complain if there's one less mouth to feed? It will mean more for everyone else.

William: It isn't human.

Watson: What would you know about being human, boy?

Mary: Shame on you for knowing less about kindness than this boy who has no mother or father.

Watson: Mary, you're a thief like all these other people. I am sick and tired of your moaning. I will not be spoken to like this. You won't get any food rations today.

Mary: You call that food? Even the rats run away when they smell it.

Watson: For that comment, you will only be given half rations for the rest of the week! I wish I could go above. This place reeks.

Mary: It smells because you don't let us wash. Our clothes are full of lice. Our hair has clumped into knots. One person falls ill and the sickness spreads through the rest of us like a wildfire.

Watson: Silence, woman!

William: (*whispers to Mary*) You are so brave, Mary.

Mary: I'm just a simple woman. This man is a turnip head and needs to be told so.

Watson: I'm warning you.

William: (*now speaks loudly and confidently to Mary*) I will share my food with you. Take some of this bread.

Watson: You're a fool, boy! Don't be taken in by her.

Mary: You're skin and bones, William. You need the food more than I do. But I'll take just the crust, if it will make you feel better.

William: I am stronger than I look. Back in London, I was the quickest to climb a chimney. My master said I was like a monkey.

Watson: Ha! You look like one, too.

Mary: I saw a monkey at a fair once. You are nothing like one, but you do remind me of my brother when we were children. After my master died last year, the household had no money to pay for a cook. I was turned out onto the street with nothing but the clothes on my back. I went to find my brother. He was my only family.

William: What happened?

Mary: I walked for three weeks. When I arrived at the village where he lived, I was half-starved. The neighbours told me he'd died of fever. I begged for work and food, but no one would help. I stole two loaves of bread, a bottle of drink and a wheel of cheese. For that crime, I am now on this voyage to the other side of the world.

Watson: Well, at least you get fed on this journey. England did you a favour.

William and Mary ignore Watson.

William: What do you think the new land will be like, Mary?

Mary: It will be better than being cooped up on this ship.

Watson: You should be thankful, Mary. One day you might be able to walk freely on land again. You could have been stuck in Newgate Prison for the rest of your life.

William and Mary again ignore Watson.

Mary: What are your hopes for the new land, William?

William: What I wish for most in this world is a full stomach and a peaceful place to work.

Mary: Perhaps we will discover some fairness in the world after all. William, I have been thinking. When we get to the new land, let's stay together. We could tell everyone that you are my adopted son.

William: I would like that.

Mary: You know I am a baker. I could teach you everything I know, if you like. They might let us both work as bakers.

William: I'd love that, Mary! We can work with the smell of fresh bread around us every day.

Watson: Ha! Instead of being covered in soot, you'll be covered in flour and yeast!

Mary: Don't mind him, William. With my recipes and your nimble hands, neither of us would ever be hungry again. And just maybe, one day we will be free and we could open our very own bakery. You could even start your own family.

William: That will take a long time, Mary, but I believe you're right. We would make a wonderful team. And if I have children of my own, I'll make sure they do not have to sweep chimneys. They might even become ladies and gentlemen and wear fine, clean clothes.

Watson: Don't dare to believe that you might ever be more than miserable thieves.

Mary: That's where you're wrong. You might be able to take away our food ...

William: ... but you can't take our dreams.